Eternally

Gluten-Free

A Cookbook of Sweets and

Inspiration, From a Teen!

Dominick Cura

Dominick Cura

Library of Congress Number
2012907107
ISBN: 0615570542
ISBN-13: 978-0615570549

To all my friends and family who enjoyed my baking and kept encouraging me. Thank you so much. You are all amazing people!

TABLE OF CONTENTS

Acknowledgements

Publishing a book is challenging, and requires hard work and dedication to see it through. It also requires the support of friends and family.

Thank you Ming Platt for helping me test some of my recipes.

Thank you to "The Pastried"- a baking group made up of me and three of my friends. Together we baked, sold pastries to friends and made some baking videos. You guys are fun I'm glad to be part of it! Special thanks to Charlie Tadlock from "The Pastried" for helping me test a few recipes.

Thank you to my mom, Marilyn Cura, for constantly running to the store to buy all the ingredients I needed and on researching how to get this book published.

Thank you to my dad, Hector Cura for taking the pictures of all the foods I baked.

Thank you Ellie Paris, another "Celiac" who gave me good feedback on my story.

I also want to give a special thanks to Matthew Amster- Burton, author of "Hungry Monkey", who edited my entire book.

Introduction

What is baking? Baking is… fun! Fun, yes, but not always easy, especially when you're baking gluten-free recipes. That's why I created some gluten-free recipes to share with you, so you don't have to go through all the work of creating your own recipes. This book is all about gluten-free sweets. I'm also going to include my story of living with Celiac Disease, and I am hoping to encourage you a lot in the story. Here are important tips to know before baking from this book:

> ➢ An important method which is used often in this book is the creaming method. This method involves mixing fat and sugar together by beating it until it's light and creamy. This process aerates the mixture, creating small bubbles, and turning the mixture into a leavening agent.

> ➢ When making a recipe which states to flour a rolling pin or surface, always flour it with tapioca flour not only to keep dough from sticking but also because it is powdery and clings to the rolling pin better than other flours.

> Here's a list of common ingredients that you will need for the recipes in this book:

  o Eggs
  o Vanilla extract
  o White Rice flour
  o Tapioca Flour
  o Baking Powder
  o Salt
  o Granulated Sugar
  o Xanthan Gum
  o Butter

> There's also another important ingredient in gluten-free baking: Xanthan gum. Xanthan gum is used as a thickening agent in foods without wheat. Gluten (like it sounds) makes everything stick together, but since we can't have gluten we use Xanthan gum to make the food stick together so it won't crumble. You especially need Xanthan gum in cookies but don't need them in foods like brownies because they are so dense.

Then there are the flours. I love gluten-free baking, because in gluten-baking you normally only use all-purpose flour, but when you are baking gluten-free you get to decide among different flours, like white rice flour, garbanzo flour, tapioca flour, corn flour, almond flour, and more. A great brand is Bob's Red Mill which has a wide variety of flours. A good store to get flours including Bob's Red Mill is at Whole Foods or other natural food stores.

Aside from the recipes I've created, I have a short story that I am hoping to inspire you with. Now you're ready to go start baking!

Life with Celiac

Before I changed my diet completely to gluten-free there was a lot of stuff going on in my life. Some good stuff, some annoying bad stuff.

My family and I had just moved to New York City from Seattle, I was two and a half years old. The winters in New York would be really cold but I liked them better than the hot summers.

Even though the summers were too hot for me, I loved the Mr. Softee ice cream trucks because of their delicious ice cream. Every summer day in the late afternoon, I would hear the music of a Mr. Softee Ice Cream Truck coming down my block. I remember I'd stop everything I was doing, run straight to my room, check my Mickey Mouse piggy bank for money and if I didn't have enough there, I would run to my parents and plead for money as fast as possible. My heart was always beating so hard because I was scared I would miss the ice cream truck. Usually kids would line up at the truck which gave me plenty of time to get my shoes on and run to the truck, but I would still rush.

I remember my favorite ice cream was vanilla ice cream in a cone which was dipped in cherry sauce. The sauce would harden forming a shell around the ice cream. I think it was called the Red Marlin, it was so delicious!

After living in New York a while, I developed Croup (Croup is a breathing difficulty accompanied by a "barking" cough). I remember my father taking me into the bathroom full of hot steam or outside into the cold New York air to reduce the swelling in my airway. Sometimes he even had to take me to the emergency room where they would give me a steroid shot to help me breathe again. There were so many nights where I barely got any sleep. Later I developed asthma.

Lots of times I'd have to sit with a big machine called a nebulizer. Medicine would be put into this machine and I would breath it in with the mask I had to wear. After the treatment I could breathe better. It was very frustrating to have to do this, and very boring because all I could do was just sit with a mask on my face next to the nebulizer for a long time!

A year before I moved to Seattle I wanted to learn to play the cello. I wanted to play the cello because it looked like a really amazing instrument and it wasn't too low or high in pitch, just right for a five year old like me. I also wanted to play it because it rhymed with Jell-o.

Later on as I played it, I learned that it really was a great instrument because it sounded so nice. I eventually got lessons and with the music I learned I started playing for my family. My aunts, uncles, and grandparents would come over my house and they would all sit on the couch and I'd just play the cello like a mini-concert. It was so fun! I loved to perform in front of everyone no matter if I was prepared or not. I was really happy playing for my family who happily listened to my music.

Then my dad found work in Seattle, Washington, we moved there when I was seven. At first I wanted to go back to New York because most of our family lived there and I was used to New York City. However in time, I eventually came to love Seattle. I realized I loved the amazing snow-capped mountains that you could see on a clear day. I started skiing and hiking in the mountains which was very fun.

However there were many things I still missed from New York. I missed my family in New York. The holidays were not the same. In New York, our family would always join us for Thanksgiving Dinner. I loved these dinners, they were always so much fun.

I also loved all the food my family made. They would make crepes, rice balls, frittata and other foods both Argentinean and Italian. The food was so delicious.

I also missed eating food from Faicco's an Italian Salumeria in Dyker Heights, Brooklyn. This place had a deli, meat department, and sold a lot of delicious Italian products. They had these frozen lemons with frozen custard inside. My mouth waters thinking of eating one of their Tortonis - ice cream made of heavy cream and eggs, topped with minced almonds and a Maraschino cherry. Whenever I visit I always go there to buy one, because they are so good!

In Seattle, I kept on playing cello and liked music even more. I joined an orchestra, but before I could join, I learned I had to audition. The auditions were scary at first. However, later I realized that auditioning wasn't really as scary or worrisome as much as having to wait for the results of the audition in the mail. That was a few years ago, today after all the auditions I've gone through, I am no longer scared.

As I was growing up in Seattle, I would get these terrible leg pains I felt in my bones. It would happen a lot but mostly at night and it caused me many sleepless nights. I felt tired all the time and had dark bags under my eyes. My mom felt there was something wrong with me because of the way I looked.

I remember that a little before I got diagnosed with Celiac Disease I was at the store with my mom. I ran across some pasta and it said, "Gluten-free." I thought what is that crazy word? I asked my mom, and she had no idea. Sure enough some time later I was diagnosed with Celiac. I always thought how coincidental and funny that was.

My pediatrician helped to diagnose my leg pain. After many tests, he eventually thought it could be Celiac Disease. He had me take yet another blood test, which was followed by a biopsy of my intestines. This type of biopsy is performed under general anesthesia. The surgeon removed tissue from my intestine and searched it for the disease. I never want to have to go through something like that again. But if I hadn't done the biopsy I wouldn't have known I have Celiac, and all of this amazing stuff which you will read about later wouldn't have happened.

If you suspect you might have Celiac you need to look into getting tested, but do not go on a gluten-free diet before the test as this will affect the results. Once diagnosed with Celiac Disease, it is very important to go on a gluten-free diet because gluten can really hurt your body. One negative effect of this disease is that your body may not be absorbing enough of the nutrients it needs.

Some information about Celiac Disease is that it is a genetic disorder, 1 in 133 people have it, and it is completely curable if you stop eating gluten. Here is a list of some common symptoms:

- Diarrhea
- Abdominal bloating or cramping
- Joint pains
- Anemia
- Being tired a lot
- Weight loss
- Vomiting
- Arthritis
- Depression
- Seizures
- Osteoporosis

If you have some of these symptoms then contact your physician and ask him or her about getting tested for Celiac Disease. This starts with a blood test.

A few weeks after my biopsy the result came in the mail. The question: "Did I have Celiac or not?" was about to be answered... I had Celiac Disease! I felt terrible.

It was hard to accept the diagnosis, because I found that almost everything I saw and wanted to eat had gluten in it and I could no longer have it. I felt so mad that I had to change my whole lifestyle.

It was also very weird because I had a disease, which sounds so much more major than just having an allergy or intolerance of some food. I was horrified.

It was like living in another world where you have no knowledge whatsoever of how you can make it through the day without gluten. Whenever I got hungry I remember thinking "What can I eat?" I would get so frustrated. It seemed like I couldn't eat anything anymore.

The beginning was difficult. We would always have to look up an ingredient we never heard of, to make sure it was gluten-free. We even had to make phone calls to the companies to double check ingredients. We realized that we had to start paying close attention to the ingredient labels. We learned about glutinous ingredients like Dextrin, Hydrolyzed Plant Protein (HPP) and

Fu. Along with gluten-free ingredients like Sodium Hexametaphosphate, Malic Acid, Glutamine, Glutinous Rice Flour (despite it's name), Buckwheat, modified food starch, and others.

If my family and I went somewhere like the mall, I had no idea what to eat. My father would always end up buying me ice cream for lunch. Of course, I was okay with that!

Happily, something nice happened to me after I was diagnosed. I found out about a place - University of Chicago Celiac Disease Center - that will send you a "care package." I thought that was great! My "care package" had some brochures, gluten-free food and even a stuffed animal. Their website is in the reference section of this book.

I was diagnosed with Celiac Disease in 2008 when I was in fourth grade. In school we would have snacks, like Goldfish crackers, which I could not have. On the days I had forgotten my "special" snack at home, I remember having to wait for my class to finish eating their gluten filled snacks while I had no snack to eat.

I would feel left out and envious of the other kids who could enjoy the snacks. After my teachers found out about my diagnosis they started to get snacks I could eat - like popcorn - just for me. This made me feel happy and special. Some of my friends would get jealous and I would tell them, "You know, if you became gluten-free then you could have these snacks too!"

One especially nice thing was, whenever someone had a party for whatever reason in school, some of my class mates would bring me something gluten-free, so I could eat too. Some people actually called me to see what I can eat. One person went out of their way and made something gluten-free for the whole class!

When I go to my friends' or family's homes, they always make sure that they have something gluten-free for me to eat. It makes me so happy to know that people are willing to do that.

It also makes me feel happy when I find a gluten-free restaurant or one with a gluten-free menu. People are so nice to do these things. Remember, always thank people at restaurants who have gluten-free menus or food, and hopefully they won't stop serving it.

In order to avoid cross-contamination with my family's food and mine I had to have a separate toaster for my bread. Do you know what that means? That's right, it's just mine and no one else's!

Having my own toaster meant that even though everyone needed to share their toaster or food in the pantry, I didn't need to. I couldn't share even if I wanted to!

Many times I would find my younger brother eating my gluten-free cookies, because, as he described it, "They are yummy!" I ended up having to hide my gluten-free cookies from my little brother, otherwise I would have no snack to eat.

The year I was diagnosed with Celiac Disease our friend Judy introduced us to Gluten-Free Girl (Shauna James Ahern). Shauna has also been diagnosed with Celiac Disease. She's an author who blogs about gluten-free cooking and has written a few gluten-free cook books.

Shauna came to my house with her family to meet with me. She agreed to co-present with me to my fourth grade class about Celiac Disease.

During my presentation I handed out brochures with information about Celiac Disease. My classmates got to try Shauna's own gluten-free cookies and some gluten-free treats from various companies. I loved teaching my class about Celiac Disease and spreading awareness of it. One of my classmates even said that we should go on a field trip to get a blood test to see if they might have Celiac!

Going on vacations were hard at first. My mom always had to research where to eat and what I could eat. Eventually we visited places in which it was very easy to eat gluten free. We visited Disney World, and this great resort outside of Seattle, Sleeping Lady Mountain Resort. Sleeping Lady didn't have okay gluten-free food, they had GREAT tasting gluten-free food, that amazed me!

A little after I was diagnosed I started my own blog and I wrote about updates in the gluten-free world. My gastroenterologist passed on information about my blog to newly diagnosed children to help them. You can find a link to my blog in the back of this book. I love having a blog because I get to share my experiences with people.

In the summer of 2011 I started baking. I decided to start baking after going to a book store and coming across a gluten-free cookbook that had great easy gluten-free recipes I found very appealing. I started making recipes from this book.

Later I tried making my own recipes by looking at different types of baked goods and learning the different methods used to make them. For example, the cake method and creaming method. I learned tips about how to use certain ingredients and the science of how they work, like for example the difference between baking soda and baking powder.

I enjoyed sharing my baked goods as much as I enjoyed playing the cello for my family. Everyone enjoyed my baking and it made me happy. I loved making my family happy with yummy gluten-free food so I thought why not make other people happy as well. I decided to write a cookbook to provide yummy gluten-free recipes to people who have Celiac Disease.

Many people are sad because they feel something may be holding them back. That's how I felt at first when I was diagnosed with Celiac Disease. In this little story I wanted to show everyone that *the worst in life isn't always the fall of happiness*.

I was devastated when I got diagnosed with Celiac Disease. It seemed like I couldn't eat anything anymore. But, as I got a little older, I started thinking about my life and realized that bad stuff that happens doesn't have to hold you back. So whenever I feel sad or mad about anything I tell myself that it won't stay like that forever, it will get better.

I learned to live happily with Celiac Disease because I created my own gluten-free blog which allowed me to write about Celiac Disease and share my feelings and ideas with everyone. I believed I could make people feel better, and this made me feel better.

I'm not saying living with Celiac Disease is really easy. It's still very hard to live with Celiac Disease. It's not easy to have to turn down a cake from a birthday party or not eat the delicious smelling pastries that tempt you. I'm usually really happy but I do get envious sometimes of people eating gluten foods.

People might think that having Celiac Disease is the end of the world, but it's actually the beginning of a new world.

I have more dreams and plans for my life, than before the diagnosis. In 7th grade, three of my friends and I created a website dedicated to baking gluten-free foods. We began filming baking videos which are on the internet. We also sold pastries to our friends.

At first it seemed like I could never eat anything good ever again. But I was wrong, having Celiac isn't the end of the world, and I discovered new delicious foods to eat. Having Celiac Disease inspired me to follow and accomplish my dreams like writing this book.

Life isn't unfair, it's just unfair for the people who choose to make it unfair! Which means that you can make choices in your life to make it turn out good but if you don't make the right choices or attempt to change your life it will stay how it is and not get better.

Celiac Disease taught me to take control of my life and to make it what I want it to be. It also made me think a lot more about my future. I should start to work for my future early in life rather than later and that *there is an opposite bright side for every dark side to life.* I have so many dreams and I know with skill, hard work and perseverance I will achieve them.

There's a difference in having a dream and making your dream come true. Anyone can dream, but if all you do is dream without putting effort into achieving your dream, then your dreams won't come true.

When I am older I want to be a movie director, but I don't think that it will just happen on its own when I'm old enough, it takes work. I thought "why not start working and learning about movie directing when I'm younger?" So I decided to teach myself about it. I have written some scripts, learned about filming techniques, and how to edit movies using movie making software. I then sharpened my skills by filming a couple of short films and cooking videos with some friends.

I hope this short story taught you that something that is bad in life can turn into something good. Don't let one problem, small or big take you down. You just have to know that your life won't stay bad unless you make it stay bad. You can get past difficult things in your life AND have a fabulous life. Go ahead!

Small Treats

Small treats, but big delicious flavor. These are usually the easiest to bake. Just remember when making gluten-free cookies you will almost always need to use Xanthan gum so that your cookies don't crumble.

Flourless Peanut Butter Cookies

These cookies are super easy to make and great if you need lots of cookies because the ingredients are so simple. Melted chocolate is a great "frosting" for these cookies.

1 large egg
¾ cup granulated sugar
2 cups peanut butter
1 tablespoon maple syrup (optional)

Preheat oven to 350 degrees F.

Mix all of the ingredients together. Then spoon the batter onto a greased pan and flatten with a spoon.

Bake for 15 minutes.

Makes about 24 cookies.

Variation: Try using another type of nut butter, like almond butter or adding some Nutella to the nut butter mixture.

Nutty Almond Cookies

These are yummy cookies and are no-bake but there is still heat involved because you will need your stovetop. These cookies are delicious and easy!

½ cup butter
1 ½ cup granulated sugar
¼ cup cocoa powder
½ cup slightly crushed pecans
½ cup almond butter
2 teaspoons vanilla extract

In a small saucepan bring the butter, sugar and cocoa powder to a boil stirring constantly while boiling. Then continue to boil and stir for about a minute. Stir in the slightly crushed pecans.

Take the mixture off the heat and stir in the almond butter and vanilla. Drop a spoonful of batter on wax paper and let cool for at least half an hour.

Makes about 15 cookies.

Alfajores

These cookies are no bake, no flour and no mess--well, not unless you drop the powdered sugar. These cookies only have three ingredients. The filling is dulce de leche, which is a thick caramel spread popular in Argentina. You can find it at almost any latino supermarket or in the ethnic section of your local grocery store.

1 T dulce de leche
2 shortbread cookies   (diameter of 3")
Some powdered sugar

Spread the dulce de leche on a shortbread cookie. Place the other cookie on top.

Dust the sandwich with powdered sugar.

Makes one sandwich cookie.

Gingerbread Cookies

Gingerbread cookies... they are so delicious and fun. Whether you like that sweet gingery taste, shaping them or frosting them these are always a delicious treat.

1 cup white rice flour
½ cup sweet rice flour
¾ cup tapioca flour
1 teaspoon baking soda
1 teaspoon salt
¼ teaspoon grated nutmeg
¾ teaspoon cinnamon

1 teaspoon salt
1 ½ teaspoon ground ginger
¾ teaspoon Xanthan gum
¾ teaspoon allspice
1 cup granulated sugar
½ cup butter
½ cup molasses
1 egg yolk

Put all the dry ingredients except the sugar in a bowl.

Cream the sugar and butter together until it is smooth. Mix in the molasses and the egg yolk and continue to mix until combined. Add in the dry ingredients and mix with an electric mixer on medium-low until it is pliable enough to roll into a ball without crumbling. Cover with cling wrap and chill for one hour.

Preheat oven to 350 degrees F. Take out a piece of plastic wrap double the size of the dough and flour it. Put the dough on it and fold it over so it's like a book and the dough is the inside pages of the book. Then, with a rolling pin, roll it out to 1/8 inch thick. At this point you can cut out any shapes or just use a cookie scoop for traditional cookies and place on an ungreased cookie sheet.

 Bake for about 10 minutes until browned more than it was already. Let cool completely and then put on frosting if you like (recipe on page 99).

Makes about 20 cookies

Panna Cotta

Panna Cotta (cooked cream) is an easy to make, Italian dessert from Piedmont in Italy. It is very good to make and to me tastes like whipped cream.

½ cup sugar
3 cups heavy cream
1 packet gelatin
¼ cup milk
1 teaspoon vanilla extract

Put milk in a small bowl, sprinkle the gelatin over it and let sit.

Combine the sugar and heavy cream in a large saucepan over high heat. Once the sugar is dissolved, boil the mixture but be careful because when it boils it immediately starts to rise.

While stirring the mixture, lower the heat to simmer and stir in the gelatin and vanilla. Pour into ramekins or cups. Cover with cling wrap and place in the refrigerator for about four hours or until it is set.

Makes about 6 small panne cotte.

Lemon Bars

These are delicious. The sourness and the sweetness are just a perfect match. They are very soft and have a burst of flavor in your mouth.

Crust:
1 cup white rice flour
1 cup tapioca flour
½ cup sugar
½ teaspoon baking soda
½ teaspoon salt
¼ cup softened butter
1 egg
1 ½ tablespoon lemon juice

½ cup vanilla yogurt
¼ cup milk

Filling:
½ cup lemon juice
2 eggs
¼ cup milk
1 cup sugar
1/4 cup tapioca flour
1/4 cup white rice flour
½ cup yogurt

Mix the dry ingredients together. Cut in the butter, then add the wet ingredients and mix until combined with a fork.

Pour into a lightly greased 9x13 inch pan. Then refrigerate for at least 15 minutes.

Preheat your oven to 350 degrees F.

Mix all the ingredients together and whisk until combined. Then pour it over the filling and bake for 25-30 minutes.

Makes about 20 bars.

Nutty Spice Muffins

These muffins are great because of the texture with the nuts and the flavor from the spices mixed together.

¾ cup white rice flour

½ cup tapioca flour

¾ teaspoon Xanthan gum

¾ teaspoon baking soda

¾ cup brown rice flour

¾ cup sugar

½ cup brown sugar

1 teaspoon cinnamon

¾ teaspoon cocoa powder

¼ teaspoon nutmeg

½ teaspoon allspice

½ cup butter

¼ teaspoon salt

3 eggs

¾ teaspoon vanilla extract

½ cup crushed almonds

½ cup crushed pecans

1 teaspoon honey

Preheat the oven to 350 degrees F.

Put the white rice flour, tapioca flour, Xanthan gum, baking soda, brown rice flour in a small bowl.

Cream the butter, salt and two sugars. Beat in the eggs and vanilla. Slowly pour in the flour mixture while mixing. If it gets too dry and is hard to beat then add in some milk.

Combine the nuts, cocoa powder, spices and honey in another bowl and then pour into the batter and mix until they are combined.

Pour into a muffin tin and bake for 20-23 minutes.

Makes about a dozen muffins.

Cakes

Cakes. Amazing sweets. These are big, delicious and decorative. There are so many varieties of cakes, they are all tasty and fun to make. Some and most of these cakes you can transform into a cupcake by just putting it in muffin tins.

Ice Cream Pie

I love ice cream! But sometimes you need to do something new with ice cream, so why not try ice cream pie! It's cold, sweet, and easy to make! Who knew this pie would be so easy!

1 ¼ cup plain crackers
2 tablespoons sugar
2 tablespoons brown sugar
4 tablespoons melted butter
¾ cup vanilla ice cream
1 tablespoon caramel sauce (optional)

Preheat the oven to 375 degrees F.

Smash the crackers in a large bowl or in a food processor until you get coarse crumbs. Then add the two sugars and melted butter. Put the crackers on a 9" pie plate and press it down all over the pie plate.

Bake it for 20 minutes. Once the pie crust has cooled down pour the ice cream over the pie crust and flatten out.

Top with caramel sauce then place in freezer and freeze until hardened.

Makes one 9 inch pie

Variation: Use other types of ice cream. You could use caramel swirl ice cream and have a different topping? Be creative, this recipe can easily be changed!

Crunchy Crumble with Cream Cheese Topping

The "Crunchy Crumble" is very good. It has a nice taste from the almond meal and cornmeal. The turbinado cane sugar gives the crumble it's sweet crunchiness. The cream cheese topping on top finishes this treat perfectly. It makes it much more refreshing than an original crumble. You can use any berries you want, frozen or fresh.

Filling:
3 cups berries
2 tablespoons sugar
½ tablespoon lime juice
1 teaspoon orange zest

½ cup almond meal
¼ teaspoon salt
¼ teaspoon ginger
½ teaspoon cinnamon
¼ cup sugar
¼ cup turbinado raw cane sugar
1 ½ tablespoon cream cheese

Crumble:
¼ cup tapioca flour
¼ cup cornmeal
¼ cup brown rice flour

Preheat your oven to 350 degrees F.

Combine the berries, sugar, orange zest, and lime juice and stir until the berries are coated.

Sift together the almond meal, tapioca flour, cornmeal, brown rice flour, sugar, salt, ginger and cinnamon in a large bowl. Stir in the cane sugar. Add in the cream cheese and butter. Then cream it until crumbs.

Pour the berries into a 8x6 container. Sprinkle the crumble mixture over the berries. Bake for 30 until the crumble is hard. Top with cream cheese topping (recipe on page 100)

Makes six servings.

Carrot Cupcakes

Carrot cake is so delicious. I never thought I would like a cake with something like carrots in it! But it surprisingly is one of my favorite sweets. The only hard part of this recipe is grating the carrots, it can take a long time!

½ teaspoon salt
1 ¾ tablespoon cinnamon
¼ teaspoon allspice
1 cup brown rice flour
1 cup white rice flour
2 teaspoons baking soda
¾ teaspoon Xanthan gum

2 ½ cups grated carrots or 6 large carrots
½ cup brown sugar
4 eggs
¾ cup buttermilk
1 ½ cup sugar
1 cup vegetable oil
1 teaspoon vanilla extract

Preheat oven to 350 degrees F.

Combine the salt, spices, flours, baking soda and Xanthan gum.

Mix the carrots and brown sugar together.

Beat the eggs, buttermilk, sugar and oil with an electric mixer on medium until combined and smooth. Beat in the vanilla and then beat in the dry ingredients until smooth and combined. Then add in the carrot mixture and mix a little longer until incorporated. Pour in cupcake tin and bake for 25 minutes.

Makes about 2 dozen cupcakes.

Pound Cake

A pound of flavor. This is an easy recipe and makes a very rich delicious smooth cake. The cake is very good with the lemon glaze on top

12 oz butter (1 ½ sticks)
1 ½ cup sugar
4 eggs
¾ vanilla extract
1 cup white rice flour
½ cup tapioca flour
½ teaspoon Xanthan gum
½ cup sour cream
¼ teaspoon salt
¼ teaspoon baking soda

Preheat the oven to 325 degrees F.

Cream the butter and sugar until light and fluffy. Add the eggs one at a time while beating with an electric mixer on medium-high. Add the vanilla then the rest of the ingredients and continue to beat until combined and smooth.

Pour into a greased 9x5 inch loaf pan and bake for 1 hour. Top with lemon glaze (recipe on page 101)

Makes one 9x5 inch pound cake.

Ricotta Cheesecake

This soft cheesecake is very delicious with ricotta cheese instead of cream cheese. It has a nice rich flavor and a great texture, I'm sure you will enjoy this cake.

Crust:

1 ½ cups smashed plain crackers
6 tablespoons melted butter
¼ cup sugar

Filling:

2 cups low-fat ricotta cheese
½ cup sugar
3 tablespoons milk
1 teaspoon vanilla extract
1 tablespoon lemon juice
3 eggs
½ tablespoon orange zest

Preheat the oven to 400 degrees F.

Mix together the crackers, melted butter and sugar then press into a 10 inch spring form pan.

Boil enough water to fit in a roasting pan (for later use).

Push the ricotta cheese through a strainer to make it smoother. Put in the vanilla, eggs, sugar, lemon juice, orange zest and milk. Whisk until a thick liquid. Pour it into the pan over the crackers.

Put on top of some aluminum foil and put in a roasting pan. Pour in the boiling water until it is half point of the spring form pan.

Bake for 1 ½ hours or until it is set. Let it cool then take out the pan and slice.

Makes one 10 inch cheesecake.

Spiced Cake

This cake has a great delicious flavor from the spices and the smooth cream cheese frosting. This cake also isn't really that hard and there aren't any hard to find ingredients. This is one of my favorites, go ahead try a slice!

½ cup butter (1 stick)
¾ cup sugar
3 eggs
¾ cup brown rice flour
1 cup white rice flour
¾ cup tapioca flour
¾ teaspoon baking powder
¾ teaspoon Xanthan gum

1 tablespoon brown sugar
½ teaspoon allspice
1 teaspoon cinnamon
¼ teaspoon ground ginger
¾ teaspoon nutmeg
½ teaspoon salt
1 teaspoon vanilla extract
¾ cup milk

Preheat oven to 350 degrees F.

Combine the dry ingredients.

Cream the butter and sugar. Add the eggs and mix with electric mixer on medium until combined but still a liquid. Combine the milk and vanilla then alternately pour little portions of the milk mixture and the dry ingredients while mixing the batter on medium-high.

Pour into a greased 9x13 pan. Then bake for about 20 minutes. Frost with cream cheese frosting (recipe on page 99).

Makes one 9x13 inch cake.

Tres Leches Cake

This is a cake from Latin America that is very tasty. This cake is called tres leches cake(three milk cake) because after you bake the cake you soak it in evaporated milk, condensed milk, and heavy cream. This is a delicious cake, that you will definitely love.

¾ cup white rice flour
¾ cup sweet rice flour
½ cup tapioca flour
½ teaspoon Xanthan gum
¾ teaspoon baking soda
¼ teaspoon salt
5 egg yolks

1 cup sugar
5 egg whites
¼ cup milk
1 teaspoon vanilla extract
1 can (14 oz) condensed Milk
1 can (12 fl oz) evaporated Milk
½ cup heavy cream

Preheat the oven to 350 degrees F.

Mix the flours, baking soda, salt and Xanthan gum together. Beat the egg yolks and sugar together with an electric mixer on medium until smooth. Fold in the flour mixture in portions of thirds with a plastic spatula until the yolks are dry. In another bowl beat the egg whites, milk and vanilla. Then mix it into the flour-egg yolk mixture until combined by hand gently with the plastic spatula again.

Pour into a greased 10 inch circle pan and bake for 30 minutes.

Mix the condensed milk, heavy cream and evaporated milk together until the condensed milk is no longer thick, then chill it in your fridge. Cool the cake and take it out of the pan. Once it's cooled place it into a larger pan.

Pour the tres leches mixture over the cake. Keep spooning the liquid over it. Finish the cake by frosting with whipped cream (recipe on page 99).

Makes one 9x13 inch cake.

Difficult (Delicious) Pastries

These, I think, are the hardest things to bake, especially when you make it gluten-free. You have to make sure it's stretchy, which is hard without gluten. But even though they are hard to make, they are still really tasty. I couldn't help myself to have two more Italian recipes in this book which are in this section. Also, some of these recipes include yeast which makes your pastry take longer to prepare because it has to sit and rise for an hour.

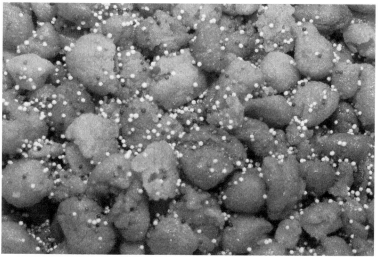

Green Tea Macarons

These are macarons not macaroons. No coconut here. But don't be sad, because these tiny treats are delicious and fun to make. Green tea powder is a little uncommon but can be found at almost every Asian market and in some American markets too. This is a very fragile cookie, make sure to follow each instruction exactly.

1 ½ cup confectioner's sugar
3 teaspoons green tea powder
1 cup almond meal
3 egg whites
1/3 cup granulated sugar

Preheat the oven to 350 degrees F.

Sift together the confectioner's sugar, green tea powder and almond meal (yes, it does ball up so what I do is sift it and stab it with a fork. I usually end up with some unbreakable bits which I throw away.)

Beat the egg whites together with an electric mixer on high until foamy. If you beat the egg whites in a plastic bowl they won't get beaten correctly and the recipe will not work, so use a metal bowl. Slowly beat in the granulated sugar with an electric mixer and keep beating until stiff and glossy. Add half of the almond flour mixture and fold it together until combined with a plastic spatula, do the same with the other half. Make sure that you have parchment paper on the baking sheet and that you have another sheet underneath the one with the parchment paper. Pipe out the batter into 1 inch circles 1 inch apart. Let sit for 10-15 minutes or until a soft skin forms on top of the macarons.

Bake for 10 minutes but stick a wooden spoon in the oven door to keep the oven a little open. Let cool. Then make frosting (recipe on page 99) but add in 1 teaspoon of green tea powder. Squeeze frosting onto cookie and top it with another cookie.

Makes about a dozen 1 inch cookies.

Pretzels

These are doughy treats that can be sweet or savory. One of the possible origins of these treats is that an Italian monk made pretzels as a reward for children who learned their prayers. The pretzels resemble the arms of a child praying.

1 teaspoon sugar
2 tablespoons warm water

2 ¼ cups white rice flour
2 cups tapioca flour
1 ½ teaspoons Xanthan gum

¼ cup sugar
1 teaspoon salt
2 egg yolks
½ cup melted butter
1 cup water

½ cup baking soda
4 cups water

In a small bowl mix the yeast, sugar, and warm water and let sit for about ten minutes or until creamy. In another bowl, combine the dry ingredients.

Make a little hole in the center and add the yeast mixture. Collapse the flour over the hole and stir with a wooden spoon until you can no longer see the yeast. Make a hole in the center of this and add the egg yolks, water and butter. Collapse the flour and then knead until stretchy.

Cover with a kitchen towel and let rise untouched for at least an hour or until it's volume has increased a little.

Preheat the oven to 450 degrees F. Take out the dough and put it on a floured surface and divide into about a dozen pieces of dough. Then roll into a rope, and form any shape you like, for the original shape of a pretzel you roll the dough out into a line then pull one side to the other side and same with the other one. The pretzels should look like the picture below .

The uncooked pretzels

Mix the water and baking soda in a small saucepan over medium heat until dissolved, then reduce heat to low. Dip each pretzel in the baking soda mixture and put onto parchment paper on top of a cookie sheet. Sprinkle with salt, then bake for 8 minutes or until browned.

Makes about a dozen pretzels.

Variation: Try stuffing the pretzels by flattening a rope of dough, stuffing it and then closing the pretzels up. But be careful when putting the pretzels in the baking soda solution.

Red Velvet Cupcakes

I love this. The rich red color is so unique! This is just an amazing recipe. In case you are wondering you have to mix together the baking soda and vinegar to make the cake smoother and have a better leavener.

½ cup shortening
½ teaspoon salt
1 ¾ cup sugar
3 eggs
2 ounces red food dye
2 tablespoons cocoa powder
1 cup buttermilk
1 teaspoon vanilla extract

1 ¾ cup white rice flour
1 cup tapioca flour
1 teaspoon Xanthan gum
1 teaspoon baking soda
2 tablespoons vinegar

Preheat the oven to 350 degrees F.

Cream the shortening, salt and sugar together. Add the eggs and beat until combined.

Make a paste by pouring red food dye on the cocoa powder in a separate bowl. Add it to the creamed mixture, and mix until it is incorporated and it is all red.

In a separate bowl combine the buttermilk and vanilla, and in another separate bowl combine the flours and Xanthan gum. While mixing the creamed mixture on medium-low pour in some of the buttermilk, then some of the flour and so on ending with the flour mixture. In a separate bowl combine the baking soda and vinegar together and fold into the cake batter.

Pour into your greased cupcake tin and bake for 30 minutes or until a toothpick comes out clean in the center.

Makes about a dozen cupcakes.

Orange Honey Buns

Honey buns are a variation of cinnamon rolls common in the southeast of United States. These aren't at all like the honey buns from the store. These make tasty buns glazed in honey, not sugar with some dough like you get from the store. Before you eat them remember they are very sticky.

Dough:

¼ cup warm water
1 packet (2 ¼ teaspoons) yeast

1 cup white rice flour
1 cup tapioca flour
1 cup brown rice flour
1/2 cup sugar
2 tablespoons butter, melted
2 eggs

1 teaspoon Xanthan gum
1/4 cup milk
1/4 teaspoon salt
½ tablespoon orange zest
2 tablespoons honey

Filling:

1 tablespoon brown sugar
4 tablespoons sugar
½ cup honey
1 tablespoon orange juice

Mix together the yeast and warm water and let sit for about ten minutes until creamy. In a large bowl combine the dry ingredients. Add in the eggs, honey, orange zest, milk and melted butter with a wooden spoon stir until doughy. Make a hole in the center and add the yeast in.

Knead with your hands until the yeast is mixed in then cover with a towel and let sit for an hour.

Preheat the oven to 350 degrees F.

Mix together all the filling ingredients until thick. Take out of the bowl and place on a floured surface. Roll out into a ¼ inch thin rectangle. Spread ¾ of the filling over the rectangle. On the long side roll up into a log and slice into about a dozen rolls then quickly place in any pan they can fit in. drizzle the rest of the honey over the rolls.

Place in the oven and bake for about 35 minutes.

Makes about a dozen buns.

Cassata Cake

Cassata cake is a Sicilian dessert served around Spring time. Cassata cake is fun to make and decorate. Fondant is a type of icing used to decorate pastries. You can make your own fondant or simply buy it at almost any baking store.

1 pound cake (recipe on page 54)
enough fondant to be rolled out and fit in a large bowl
1 ½ cups ricotta cheese
¾ cup sugar
½ cup milk
As much candied and/or dried fruits as you would like

Slice the pound cake into long pieces that will cover the whole bowl with no spaces in between. Place enough parchment paper to cover the inside of the bowl.

Put the fondant rolled out in the bowl. Then place pieces of the pound cake along the sides of the bowl. Make sure to cover up all the holes where you can see the fondant with pound cake. Don't worry if it looks messy because it will be covered up with fondant.

Pour the ricotta cheese through a strainer into a medium bowl. Add the sugar and milk. Whisk together the ricotta until it is combined and a thick liquid. Mix in the fruits then pour the ricotta over the pound cake. Cover with plastic wrap and chill in the refrigerator for at least an hour.

Unwrap the cake and invert on a plate. Then decorate with frosting, sugar pearls, or whatever you would like.

Makes one cake.

Cinnamon Rolls

Another delicious treat, full of sugar and spice! This is very fun to make, and if you've ever made sushi rolls, well, this is similar, because you roll out the dough, spread on the cinnamon, roll it up, and slice in little pieces.

Dough:

¼ cup warm water
1 packet (2 ¼ teaspoons) yeast

1 cup white rice flour
1 cup tapioca flour
1 cup brown rice flour
1/2 cup sugar
4 tablespoons butter, melted

2 eggs
1 teaspoon Xanthan gum
1/2 cup milk
1/4 teaspoon salt

Filling:

2 tablespoons melted butter
1 tablespoon cinnamon
1/4 cup brown sugar

Mix the yeast and water together. Then let sit for at least 10 minutes. Mix all of the dry ingredients together. Make a little hole in the center where you then add the wet ingredients. Collapse in the flour over the hole and with a spoon mix to combine. Mix in the yeast mixture.

Knead it with your hands and until it's all combined into one big piece of dough. Then cover it and let it sit for at least 1 hour.

Preheat the oven to 350 degrees F.

After it has risen put it onto a floured surface then knead it by just punching it. Roll it out into a rectangle. Combine the brown sugar and cinnamon. Brush the melted butter over the dough then sprinkle the cinnamon mixture over that. Starting from the long side, roll it up into a log and cut it into about a dozen rolls. Place in any pan that can hold them, then put more melted butter on them and sprinkle more filling or brown sugar.

Bake for 35 minutes.

Makes about a dozen rolls.

Variation: Add nuts or raisins in the filling

Struffoli

Struffoli are little balls of dough that are fried then dipped in honey and shaped into a dome. Struffoli are from Naples, Italy and are served around Christmas time. This Italian dessert is very beautiful and delicious. The outside is crunchy and the inside is soft. One bite and you'll love it!

Dough:
¾ teaspoon Xanthan gum
1 cup brown rice flour
1 cup white rice flour
¼ cup sugar
¼ teaspoon salt
4 tablespoons butter, sliced into pieces
3 eggs

zest of half a lemon
zest of half an orange
1 ½ tablespoon white wine

Other ingredients:
vegetable oil for frying
1 ½ cup honey
¼ cup sugar
sprinkles to decorate with

Put the dry ingredients in a bowl. Add the butter and cut and mix it together with two forks to get chunks of flour or big crumbs. Add the rest of the ingredients for the dough and continue to cream it until it is doughy. If it is too dry you can add a little more white wine.

Roll the dough into balls the size of a small marble.

Pour enough oil in a large saucepan to fill it halfway. Heat over medium- high heat. Once the oil is hot enough (you can test the heat of the oil by dropping a piece of the dough in the oil, and when it starts to become golden brown or actually cook then it's ready.) Fry the struffoli until golden brown.

Combine the honey and sugar in a saucepan over medium-high heat until the sugar is dissolved. Pour the struffoli in the honey and coat the fried struffoli in honey. Place on a plate. Form into a dome and pour sprinkles on top.

Makes about 10 servings.

Extra Sweets

This chapter has recipes for breakfast and drinks, but all are sweets! All of these recipes are very easy because who wants to waste an hour to make breakfast or drinks?

Blueberry Quinoa

Quinoa is a grain from the Andean region of south America. It can be used in a savory way or in a sweet way. This quinoa recipe is very sweet and has the great flavor of blueberries simmered into the quinoa.

1 cup quinoa
2 cups water
2 tablespoons brown sugar
½ cup blueberries
1 ½ tablespoons honey

Place the quinoa in a strainer under cold running water until no more foam appears. Pour the quinoa into a saucepan. Mix in the rest of the ingredients.

Bring to a boil. Reduce the heat and simmer, covered for 20 minutes or until water is absorbed. Serve with milk.

Makes four servings.

Variation: Experiment with quinoa and try to make your own recipe, but make sure that you always clean the quinoa, and that the amount of water is double the amount of quinoa.

Crepes

Crepes are very thin pancakes that are very light. These can be made as a savory food or sweet food. To me these are much better than regular pancakes because you can fill them with whatever you like! I remember on my dad's side of the family, everyone would make crepes or Panqueques (the Argentinean name for pancakes) and I loved eating these. Sadly, when I was diagnosed with Celiac no one knew a good way to make gluten-free crepes. Because of that I had to develop my own recipe for crepes.

1 ½ cups white rice flour
2 eggs
¼ teaspoon salt
2 tablespoons melted butter
1 cup milk
3 tablespoons sugar
¾ teaspoon vanilla

Sift the flour into a medium sized bowl. Add the sugar and salt. Beat in each egg individually then add the butter and vanilla

Lightly butter a skillet. Pour just enough batter onto the skillet so that you can spread it evenly around the pan without it being too thick. Once it starts to solidify flip it over carefully. After a bit check the underside of the crepe and once it's hard enough, take it out of the skillet. You can fill it with whatever you want: Strawberries, Nutella, sugar, anything.

Makes about a dozen large crepes (but it changes with the size of your skillet)

Pancakes

Pancakes are a great breakfast to have. They aren't too hard to make and are tasty. The sour cream (or yogurt) gives the pancakes a nice taste that isn't super sweet.

¾ cup sweet rice flour
2 cup white rice flour
¼ teaspoon salt
3 eggs
2 tablespoons canola oil
¾ cup sour cream or yogurt
1 teaspoon baking soda
1 ¼ cup milk

Sift the white rice flour and sweet rice flour into a large bowl. Then add the rest of the ingredients and whisk until combined. The batter should be light and not stick in the whisk. Put the stove on medium-high, then butter the griddle. Once the butter is melted, spoon the batter onto the griddle using about two tablespoons of batter.

Once it rises a bit and bubbles start to show, flip it over. Then when you can see it looks ready, take it off the griddle

Makes about a dozen pancakes.

Easy Smoothie

I love smoothies. They are my favorite thing ever. I try to always have a pack of berries and some yogurt in my refrigerator so that whenever I want, I can make a delicious smoothie.

About ½ cup large strawberries
½ cup vanilla yogurt
1 banana

Blend all the ingredients together on high in a blender until smooth (about a minute or two.).

Makes about two servings.

Variation: Use whatever fruits you would like.

Italian Soda

Italian soda is a soft drink that is very simple. It has flavored syrup, and you can buy whatever flavor you want, so you can vary the recipe for whatever you like.

3 tablespoons flavored syrup
Enough carbonated water to fill your cup barely to the top (leaving room for the milk)
¼ cup milk

Drop ice into a cup. Pour in the syrup then the carbonated water and pour the milk on top.

Makes one serving.

Vanilla Milkshake

Milkshakes are so easy to make. So if you are tired of just having regular boring ice cream in a bowl or cone try a milkshake. You can get any ice cream you want and make any flavor milkshake!

1 tablespoon sugar
1 cup vanilla ice cream
1/2 cup milk
1/2 teaspoon vanilla

Blend all the ingredients together on high until smooth.

Makes one serving.

Variation: Use any ice cream you want.

Hot Chocolate

I love when you're outside and it's freezing, and then you go inside your house and have some hot chocolate. The soothing feeling just makes you relax. This hot chocolate is rich and full in flavor.

2 cups milk ¼ cup granulated sugar
1 teaspoon vanilla extract
4 tablespoons cocoa powder

Warm up the milk in a small saucepan on medium-high until some bubbles form on the edges of the saucepan.

Take off the heat and mix in the other ingredients with whisk.

Makes two servings.

Lemonade

Lemonade is delicious for a hot day because it's very refreshing. For a great variation, try carbonated water instead of regular water.

1 cup water
¼ cup lemon juice
¼ cup granulated sugar

Stir all ingredients together.

Makes two servings.

Variation: Substitute water for carbonated water to get more of a "soda" lemonade.

Toppings

Sometimes that one dessert isn't enough. Here are some extra stuff to add to it to give it some more taste.

Whipped Cream

1 cup whipping cream
1 teaspoon vanilla extract
¼ cup confectioner's sugar

Beat all the ingredients with an electric mixer on high until you get stiff peaks.

Frosting Recipe

½ cup butter (at room temperature)
1 teaspoon vanilla extract
¼ teaspoon salt
2 cups confectioner's sugar
2 tablespoons milk

Mix the butter and vanilla together with an electric mixer on medium. Add in the sugar while mixing until fluffy, then add milk and mix with an electric mixer on medium until soft, scraping the bowl occasionally.

Cream Cheese Frosting

1 cup cream cheese
1 cups confectioner's sugar

½ cup softened butter
1 teaspoon vanilla extract

Mix cream cheese, butter and sugar and vanilla together with an electric mixer.

Cream Cheese Topping

¾ cup cream cheese
½ teaspoon vanilla
1 ½ tablespoon milk

Whisk together all the ingredients until smooth.

Crème Fraiche

1 cup whipping cream
2 tablespoons buttermilk

Combine the two ingredients in a glass jar and let sit at room temperature, covered for about 12 hours or until thickened. If you want add some honey or sugar to sweeten it a bit.

Lemon Glaze

2 tablespoons lemon juice
1 teaspoon vanilla extract
1 cup powdered sugar

Mix together the lemon juice and vanilla. Then slowly whisk in the sugar until you have a smooth yellowish white glaze. Quickly pour over your cake.

Resources

My blog:
http://www.eternallyglutenfree.blog.com

National Foundation for Celiac Awareness
http://www.celiaccentral.org

National Institutes of Health (NIH),
Celiac Disease Awareness Campaign
http://www.celiac.nih.gov

University of Chicago Celiac Disease Center If
you have been diagnosed in the last 12 months
call here for a gluten-free care package:
(773) 702-7593
http://www.cureceliacdisease.org

Celiac Disease Foundation (CDF)
http://www.celiac.com

Celiac Sprue Association
http://www.csaceliacs.info

Gluten Intolerance Group Of North America
http://www.gluten.net

Celiac Disease Center at Columbia University
http://www.celiacdiseasecenter.org

Gluten-free Summer Camps for Kids

Camp Celiac
Livermore, California
http://www.celiaccamp.com

Celiac Disease Foundation Summer Camp
Studio City, California
http://www.celiac.org

Camp Weekaneatit
Warm Springs, Georgia
http://www.georgiarock.org

Camp New Hope
McGregor, Minnesota
http://www.twincitiesrock.org

Camp Aldersgate/Camp Celiac
N. Scituate, Rhode Island
http://campceliac.org

Camp Gilmont

Gilmer, Texas

http://www.dallasrock.org

GIG Kids Camp West

Vashon Island, Washington

http://campsealth.org

Two Bars Seven Ranch

Tie Siding, Wyoming

http://www.twobarssevenranch.com

Made in the USA
Charleston, SC
11 January 2013